EMOTIONAL CHECK ENGINE LIGHTS

A Scripture-Based Guide to Identify Lies, Renew Your Mind, and Walk in Obedience

Dr. Stacy Wright, PsyD, HSPP

Published by Faithful Counsel

Cover design by Dr. Stacy Wright

ISBN: 979-8-9950377-0-5

Printed in the United States of America.

To my husband: thank you. Unknowingly, you supplied grist for the mill God used in my refinement. I would never have known how sweet our Lord is had I not been placed in that fiery trial. Thank you for your patience during the writing of this book, when I was continually reminded of my great need for Him and called to practice what I preach again and again.

My prayer is that this book may help others walk in obedience, bringing glory to God and fruit to those who love Him.

Table of Contents

Search me, God, and know my heart;

test me and know my anxious thoughts.

See if there is any offensive way in me,

and lead me in the way everlasting.

Psalm 139:23-24

Check Engine Lights

Have you ever been driving down the road and suddenly your check engine light comes on? It gets your attention fast, doesn't it? It's not exactly a welcome sight, but it is helpful. Your car is alerting you that something may be wrong under the hood. Imagine if that light weren't part of the car's design. Problems could build quietly until you suddenly found yourself stranded on the side of the road. Negative emotions work a lot like that. They're like check engine lights on the dashboard of the soul.

In my practice, I see all kinds of emotions, most of them negative. People usually don't come to counseling because life is going great. They come because they're anxious, angry, sad, scared, overwhelmed, or discouraged. When I call these emotions "negative," I don't mean they're bad or that we shouldn't have them. I just mean they're uncomfortable.

They're not the feel-good emotions most of us would choose. If you're like most people, when sadness, fear, depression, or anxiety show up, you want them gone as quickly as possible.

I've seen this play out over and over again in counseling. Someone keeps pushing through for months, telling herself she's fine. She stays busy, smiling and serving. She keeps functioning while ignoring the growing anxiety. She becomes more irritable and less patient with her children and spouse. As she grows increasingly exhausted, she ignores the sadness, telling herself she just needs to "get it together." Then one small conflict, one disappointment, or one more hard day hits, and suddenly she feels like she's falling apart. But she's not reacting only to that one moment. The light's been blinking for a long time.

I know that pattern not only from counseling others, but from my own life. There was a season when I lay on the floor unable to get up, and a simple sentence I had memorized— reluctantly—became the lifeline that pulled me back. I'll tell that story later. That experience changed the way I understand suffering, and it's part of why I wrote this book. I want you to know from the start: this book isn't theory for me. It was born out of suffering and out of learning firsthand how God uses painful emotions to draw us closer to Himself and change us in ways no mountaintop experience ever could.

That's one reason why Peter's words hit so hard: "Dear friends, do not be surprised at the fiery ordeal that has come on you to test you, as though something strange were happening to you" (1 Peter 4:12). Even though we all know life in this fallen world includes pain and suffering, we still tend to act shocked when it shows up in our own lives. How often have you gone through a trial and found yourself thinking, *I can't believe this is happening to me?* As irrational as it sounds when we say it out loud, most of us still live as though we expect life to go our way. And when it doesn't, we instinctively start looking for the fastest way out of the pain.

When we operate from that mindset, we start looking for a remedy—a way to get out of the negative feelings as quickly as possible and, hopefully, avoid them in the future.

But negative emotions are part of life, and many times they serve as God-given warning signals for the soul. When sadness, anger, fear, or anxiety rise up, they may be alerting us to something going on beneath the surface. They're signaling that it's time to stop and look under the hood.

We understand this principle easily when it comes to physical pain. When your body hurts, you know something may be wrong. God designed our bodies with warning systems. Pain gets your attention. It alerts you to a possible problem. Of course, people can ignore physical symptoms too, or try to numb them so they don't have to deal with what the pain may be telling them. We do the same thing with emotional pain.

I teach clients to become objective observers of their emotions, recognizing them when they arise and taking time to explore where they're coming from. Sometimes there's an external event stirring up sadness, anger, or fear—something outside their control. Other times, the emotion is being fueled by their own thinking. Either way, when a negative emotion surfaces, it's important to stop and trace it to its root.

How to Use This Book

This book is a tool. It isn't a replacement for counseling, discipleship, pastoral care, or Christian community.

Check Engine Light Journaling is designed to help you slow down, examine your inner life, and practice obedience to God's Word in real time, especially when emotions feel intense or confusing. The companion *Check Engine Light Journal* is sold separately and includes preformatted pages for the journaling process explained in this book.

This book works best between crises, not just in them. You don't need to journal every emotion or complete every step perfectly. The goal isn't mastery. It's faithfulness. The process is simple: bring what you're feeling and thinking under the authority of Scripture, then walk in obedience.

You can use this book:

- independently, as a daily or as-needed practice
- alongside counseling, to reinforce work done in session
- in discipleship, with a trusted mentor or small group
- in pastoral care, as a structured way to move from insight to action

Any of these contexts can work. This approach may be especially helpful when:

- emotions feel intense or hard to sort through
- the same thoughts keep resurfacing
- you know the truth but struggle to live like you believe it

Check Engine Light Journaling doesn't promise quick emotional relief. Sometimes obedience brings peace quickly. Sometimes it brings clarity first. But obedience always leads to life.

Use this book slowly, honestly, and prayerfully.

A Note to Counselors, Pastors, and Helping Professionals

As a licensed clinical psychologist, I wrote this book with respect for both clinical wisdom and biblical authority. Check Engine Light Journaling isn't a therapeutic modality, and it's not intended to compete with counseling. It's a practical tool to help people identify emotionally driven beliefs, expose underlying lies, confront those beliefs with Scripture, and practice faith through concrete action.

In practical terms, this process helps people slow down, get their thoughts out of their heads and onto paper, and see them clearly—which often brings both relief and insight. It can support emotional regulation, increase self-awareness, and encourage action rooted in truth rather than mood.

Spiritually, it reinforces that Scripture is the final authority, that obedience is an expression of faith, and that sanctification is a process rather than a single moment.

This tool may be especially useful for people who can identify truth intellectually but struggle to live in alignment with it. For those who often find themselves stuck between insight and action, or wrestle with anxiety, shame, anger, or fear that is often tied to distorted beliefs.

Check Engine Light Journaling isn't designed to bypass grief, trauma, or clinical complexity. It's meant to anchor the reader in truth and obedience while appropriate care continues.

My hope is that this book serves as a bridge between sessions, between sermons, and between conviction and action, helping people learn not only what they believe, but how to live like they believe it.

PART ONE:

Understanding the Dashboard

Trust in Him at all times, you people;

pour out your hearts to Him,

for God is our refuge.

Psalm 62:8

Chapter 1

When the Light Comes On

So how do we respond when the light comes on? Psalm 55:22 says, "Cast your cares on the Lord and He will sustain you; He will never let the righteous be shaken." That's not a decorative verse for a coffee mug or wall art. It's a command. We are commanded to take our emotions to God. When anger, anxiety, or sadness rise up, our first response should be to bring those emotions to Him.

We don't need polished words before we come to God. Scripture tells us that even when we don't know what to pray, "the Spirit himself intercedes for us through wordless groans"

(Romans 8:26). We'll return to this more fully later when we talk about fervent prayer and lament.

Intense emotions should drive us to the Lord, but many of us don't respond that way. Instead of slowing down, we speed up. We reach for quick fixes, distractions, addictions, escapes, or even labels that seem to explain the struggle without addressing its root. We tell ourselves, *I'll deal with this later*, but every time we don't deal with it, it's still dealing with us—showing up as low-grade worry, panic, irritability, mood swings, or deepening sadness. We hope the warning signals will go away on their own, or we try to drown them out with shallow substitutes like drugs, alcohol, work, busyness, or sexual sin.

Sometimes even a diagnosis can feel like relief. It may name the struggle, but it can also become an excuse, an identity, or permission to stay stuck. Labels may describe patterns of suffering, sin, or responses to being sinned against, but they don't get to the root. If we run to Him instead of substitutes, He promises peace. God is our refuge and strength, a very present help in trouble (Psalm 46:1).

I want to encourage you to pay attention to these warning signals. They're part of how God designed you, and although they don't feel good, they serve a good purpose. Emotions are not just thoughts floating around in your head. They involve your body too. When you're angry, you may feel your blood pressure rise. When you're anxious, your heart may start racing. When you're sad, you may feel a heaviness in your chest. Researchers have described how the brain and body work together in emotional responses, especially in fear, threat detection, arousal, and physiological activation (LeDoux, 1996; LeDoux, 2012).

That's part of why intense emotions are so hard to ignore. Like physical pain, they get your attention. And that's not a design flaw. It's part of the warning system. The problem isn't that the light comes on. The problem is when we let the light drive the car.

Painful emotions aren't detours from God's plan—they're often the very places where He intends to shape you. James wrote, "Consider it pure joy, my brothers and sisters, whenever you face trials of many kinds, because you know that the testing of your faith produces perseverance. Let perseverance finish its work so that you may be mature and complete, not lacking anything" (James 1:2–4). Every time that light flashes on your dashboard, you have the chance to stop, notice, and invite Him to do His refining work in you. Paul echoed this in Romans 5:3-4: "We rejoice in our sufferings, knowing that suffering produces endurance, and endurance produces character, and character produces hope." Not every painful emotion is rooted in sinful or distorted thinking; many are appropriate responses to living in a fallen world. Even so, every emotion still provides us an opportunity to examine what we believe and bring our response under the authority of God's Word.

But bringing emotion to God is only the beginning. Once the light has our attention, we also have to ask what it's revealing. *What am I believing right now? What am I assuming about God, myself, this person, or this situation? What story is my heart telling me?* The warning light is not meant to become the driver. It's meant to send us to God, where our thoughts, desires, and responses can be examined.

Along these same lines, Scripture also commands us to bring our thoughts under the authority of Christ. That too is a command. If we profess to love Him, we should obey what He says. Obedience is the response of those who trust that God is already at work for their good and who remember that only He can bring beauty from ashes (Isaiah 61:3).

Do not deceive yourselves.

If any of you think you are wise by the

standards of this age, you should become

"fools" so that you may become wise.

1 Corinthians 3:18

The Gold Standard Versus the Greater Standard

In the counseling world, Cognitive Behavioral Therapy, or CBT, has been called the "gold standard" of psychotherapy for decades (David et al., 2018). I was trained in it, used it, and saw that it could help—but only superficially. CBT may bring insight, structure, and even some measure of relief, but it still falls far short of real healing.

At its core, CBT teaches that our thoughts, feelings, and behavior are connected. When one shifts, the others are affected. Most often, it's our thinking that drives the rest. I often use three fingers to illustrate this with counselees: one for thoughts (index finger), one for feelings (middle finger), and one for behavior (ring finger). Tug on either the index or ring finger, and the others move too. But the "feeling finger" is stuck in the middle. You can't just command it to change directly. If you're sad, you're sad. If you're mad, you're mad, and if you're scared, you're scared. Most of us have had the experience of someone telling us to "calm down," and we all know full well that it doesn't work. Feelings don't usually respond to commands. They respond to what's driving them.

Psychological literature has also recognized this basic connection between thoughts, feelings, and behavior. The way we interpret a situation shapes the emotion that follows (Lazarus, 1991), and what people believe about a situation affects how they feel and how they respond (Beck, 1967; Harris, 1989).

When I tell people that they can't control how they feel, they look at me in disbelief. We've all come to believe that we're supposed to control our feelings. And when we can't, then we only pile more negative feelings on top of the original one, like shame and hopelessness. This only compounds our problem. It's a fact that we cannot directly control *how* we feel, but the catch is that we *can* control *what we do* with our feelings.

To illustrate this, imagine you're walking into a grocery store behind a woman and her toddler. She jerks the child by the arm, raises her voice, and calls the toddler stupid and slow. Right away, something rises up in you, maybe anger, sadness, or protectiveness. Did you choose the emotion you felt in that moment? Of course you didn't; they surged. But why? If you slow down and listen to your thoughts, you might hear something like, *That's wrong. That child shouldn't be treated that way.* Underneath that reaction is a belief: children are meant to be protected and cared for, not belittled. The feeling wasn't random. It flowed from what you believe to be true.

And yet, when it comes to our own emotions, we keep trying to control them directly. We try to shut them down, silence them, beat ourselves up over them, or override them. But if emotions were that easy to command, counseling offices wouldn't be full, addictions wouldn't have the grip they do, and so much of the pharmaceutical industry wouldn't be built around managing distress. Emotions aren't switches we flip. They're signals rooted in what we believe.

Focusing on feelings themselves won't resolve them. We have to become aware of the thoughts driving them. If you've ever spiraled with thoughts like, *What if I fail? What if no one likes me? What if everything goes wrong?* then you already know how helpful it is to slow down and put those thoughts into words. Once they're out in front of you, you can begin to examine them. That's one of the reasons CBT has helped so many people. It brings order to what feels chaotic. But eventually, a bigger question has to be asked: what exactly is "rational," and who gets to decide?

My Secular Training

Here's a good place to tell you a little bit about myself. I earned my bachelor's, master's, and doctorate in clinical psychology before I became a born-again Christian. Cognitive Behavioral Therapy (CBT) was one of the major approaches I studied and practiced all through training and later in hospitals, clinics, and eventually in my own private practice.

Back in the 1960s, psychologists Albert Ellis and Aaron Beck began noticing a pattern in their patients. Beck had been trained in psychoanalysis, the old Freudian approach, but it wasn't working. Turns out, digging up old bones and licking them isn't all that helpful. His patients weren't getting better. He noticed connections between the thought life of his patients and their moods. He started paying closer attention to what they were actually thinking—and that's where Cognitive Behavioral Therapy was born (Ellis, 1962; Beck, 1976).

CBT rightly observes that thoughts shape mood and behavior, often outside a person's awareness. What I accepted for years without much question was its underlying framework, the idea that thoughts could be sorted simply into what was "irrational" and what was "rational." It wasn't until I came into a saving relationship with the Lord that I truly began to read and study Scripture. Then one day I came across 2 Corinthians 10:5 that says, "take every thought captive and make it obedient to Christ." Those words practically jumped off the page at me. I remember thinking, *God already said this??* Long before psychology gave it a name, God had already laid out the truth. I began to see why CBT has been so helpful to so many people. It's brushing up against something real. It echoes truth, even though it doesn't begin with the Truth Himself.

As our culture has drifted further from objective truth, "rational" has become harder and harder to define. Some research has even suggested that the effects of CBT for depression have declined over time (Johnsen & Friborg, 2015). Whatever one makes of that finding, the larger issue remains: scientific theories and conclusions develop over time. That doesn't make science useless. It simply means science is always subject to revision, while God's Word is not. Scripture says, "There is a way that seems right to a man, but its end is the way to death" (Proverbs 14:12).

That's where biblical counseling is different. CBT aims for rational. Scripture calls us to truth. CBT says, "Let's replace irrational thoughts with rational ones." God says, "Take every thought captive and make it obedient to Christ" (2 Corinthians 10:5). Rational shifts with culture. Truth doesn't. Jesus prayed, "Sanctify them in the truth; Your word is truth" (John 17:17). Isaiah wrote, "The grass withers, the flower fades, but the word of our God stands forever" (Isaiah 40:8). And Jesus promised, "You will know the truth, and the truth will set you free" (John 8:32). So instead of rational versus irrational, Scripture gives us a greater standard: truth.

Up until that point, I hadn't thought much about integrating my faith into my practice. I foolishly thought I could keep my career separate from my faith. But even while I was using CBT and doing everything by the book, I was deeply dissatisfied with my work. My practice was running from a strictly secular worldview. Wright Psychological Services was where people came for testing, assessment, diagnosis, and symptom management.

When the Lord began prying my selfish fingers, one painful digit at a time, off the grip I had on my practice, He also led me to change the name to Faithful Counsel, where counseling would be anchored in truth and shaped by love. Now people weren't coming just for diagnosis and symptom management. They were coming to see themselves and God in light of His Word. My practice was flipped on its head. I was deeply intimidated and full of fear making that change, but I also felt excited about helping hurting people in a way I hadn't before. I knew the Lord was showing me the true path to freedom.

In biblical counseling, it's not my professional opinion that matters most, and it's not the client's opinion either. Together, we submit to the Word of God as the plumb line. In practice, that means when a client says, "I feel like God has abandoned me," we don't just validate the feeling—we open Scripture together and ask, "What has God actually said about that?" This process doesn't stop where CBT stops. It asks not merely whether a thought sounds reasonable, but whether that thought agrees with God's Word.

The freedom the gospel offers isn't just relief from anxious or irrational thinking. It's freedom from the power of sin itself. CBT may help identify distorted thoughts, but only the cross deals with the deeper root: the sinful heart that produces them. Jesus said, "Everyone who sins is a slave to sin… but if the Son sets you free, you will be free indeed" (John 8:34, 36).

The gospel brings freedom because Christ has already won the victory. His death paid for our guilt, and His resurrection broke sin's power. Paul wrote, "If anyone is in Christ, he is a new creation; the old has gone, the new has come" (2 Corinthians 5:17).

This kind of transformation isn't sheer willpower, positive thinking, or self-improvement. It's the Spirit of God applying the Word of God to the child of God, producing what no human system can.

But the Lord God called to the man,

"Where are you?"

Genesis 3:9

CHAPTER 3

Emotions and the Fall

When Adam and Eve sinned in the garden, emotions entered human experience in a painful new way. Before sin, their hearts and emotions were perfectly aligned with God's will. They knew only peace, joy, and unhindered fellowship with Him. But after sin, fear, shame, and blame became the first "check engine lights" on the human dashboard. Genesis 3 tells us that once they ate from the tree, "the eyes of both were opened, and they realized they were naked; so they sewed fig leaves together and made coverings for themselves" (Genesis 3:7). A few verses later, Adam confessed to God, "I was afraid because I was naked, so I hid" (Genesis 3:10).

The emotions of shame and fear that led Adam and Eve to run and hide weren't random. They were the natural consequence of a heart now bent by sin. And what was true for Adam and Eve remains true for us today. Our emotions are often signals that something is broken inside us or around us. The problem is that our fallen hearts don't always interpret those signals rightly. Left unchecked, shame drives us to hide, fear drives us to avoid, and anger drives us to blame. What feels right to the heart often pulls us further from God instead of closer to Him.

Painful emotions remind us that this world is not as it should be. Scripture says that creation itself is groaning (Romans 8:22), and we groan with it. Grief, injustice, disappointment, and longing all point to the fracture. They remind us we were made for something better, for the day when "He will wipe every tear from their eyes. There will be no more death or mourning or crying or pain" (Revelation 21:4).

We see the same struggle in our world today. We live in a culture that's obsessed with feelings, and if someone feels it, everyone is expected to validate and affirm whatever feelings they have. A teenager feels anxious about a social situation, and instead of examining the fear, she's told to avoid anything that makes her uncomfortable. A man feels angry at his wife, and instead of asking whether his expectations are reasonable, he assumes his anger proves she's wrong. Feelings are treated as ultimate truth, and people are led by them. But God's Word warns us, "Trust in the Lord with all your heart and lean not on your own understanding; in all your ways submit to him, and he will make your paths straight" (Proverbs 3:5–6). This is why we can't simply follow our hearts. They need the steadying correction of God's Word.

So how do we actually stop leaning on our own understanding? We slow down long enough to see what we're truly believing. Emotions move quickly. Thoughts flash by unnoticed. If we don't pause, we assume whatever rises first must be true. But Scripture calls us not to assume, but to examine.

When people slow down enough to listen to what their hearts are saying, those thoughts often surface as "What if" questions: *What if this goes wrong? What if I end up alone?* But those questions are not always neutral. Scripture tells us, "The heart is deceitful above all things and beyond cure. Who can understand it?" (Jeremiah 17:9). The heart has a way of disguising what it believes. Beneath *What if no one talks to me?* may be the belief, *No one will talk to me.* Beneath *What if I mess this up?* may be, *I'm going to mess this up.* This matters because what stays hidden tends to govern us. Once those beliefs are brought into the light, they can be examined against God's truth.

This is how quickly sin twists our thinking: from fear to shame, from shame to blame, and even to questioning God's goodness. The same pattern still repeats in our lives today. Fear, shame, anger, and blame are still flashing on the dashboard of the soul.

If Adam and Eve had stopped to examine what they were believing, their thoughts might have sounded familiar: *God is angry with me. He won't forgive me. I'm alone. Someone else is to blame. God shouldn't have let this happen.* But God's Word answers those fears differently: He is compassionate and gracious, faithful to forgive, and near to those who look to Him (Psalm 103:8; 1 John 1:9; Psalm 34:5).

And the same God who walked into the garden and asked, "Where are you?" still meets us in those moments, not to condemn us, but to expose the lies we're believing and replace them with His truth.

In the garden, fear and shame drove Adam and Eve into hiding. In Christ, those same warning lights can drive us out of hiding and back to God. The next question is how we obey when those thoughts rise up. That's where the next command comes in.

PART TWO:

The Practice

We demolish arguments and every pretension that sets itself up against the knowledge of God, and we take captive every thought to make it obedient to Christ.

2 Corinthians 10:5

Taking Every Thought Captive

At the heart of this practice is obedience to a clear command in Scripture: "We demolish arguments and every pretension that sets itself up against the knowledge of God, and we take captive every thought to make it obedient to Christ" (2 Corinthians 10:5). That command can feel overwhelming. How can anyone possibly take every thought captive when the mind feels like a whirlwind? When the emotional check engine light comes on, it's signaling that something in our thinking is misfiring, and that is the moment this command becomes necessary.

When I ask clients what image comes to mind when they hear the phrase "take captive," they usually picture something that doesn't want to be caught. I do too. I picture a wild animal that has roamed freely for so long that it feels at home there. It doesn't walk calmly into a cage. It resists.

Our thoughts can be like that. Some have been allowed to roam freely for years. They feel familiar. They may even feel protective. But familiar does not mean harmless. A thought can feel at home in your mind and still be destroying the garden. That's why Paul's language matters. He doesn't say to merely notice every thought, consider every thought, or make peace with every thought. He says to take it captive and make it obedient to Christ. The thought doesn't get to call the shots. The emotion doesn't get to run the show. Even my own will has to bow. Christ is Lord over this too.

This is where obedience becomes costly. Taking a thought captive often means our own will has to die. Jesus said, "Whoever wants to be My disciple must deny themselves and take up their cross daily and follow Me" (Luke 9:23). That includes the inner life. We don't get to keep thoughts, emotions, desires, or interpretations that refuse to bow to Him. Because of the Fall, our emotions are often tangled with the flesh. They may pull us toward self-protection, control, revenge, self-pity, comfort, avoidance, or pride. That doesn't mean every painful emotion is sinful. But it does mean every emotion must be submitted to Christ. The feeling may still protest. The will may still resist. But obedience says, "Not my will, but Yours."

This is the reason I created Check Engine Light Journaling. It's a practical tool that helps us realistically obey this command. It slows down the chaos in your head. It gives you a structure to capture thoughts on paper, look at them clearly, and then line them up against the truth of God's Word. As you use the Check Engine Light Journal, you'll be training yourself in obedience to the Lord's command. You'll learn to recognize and confront the thoughts you've allowed to go unexamined. Scripture warns us not to let emotion take the wheel: "Fools give full vent to their rage, but the wise bring calm in the end" (Proverbs 29:11), and "those who trust in themselves are fools, but those who walk in wisdom are kept safe" (Proverbs 28:26). The emotion may alert you, but it must not rule you.

Taking a thought captive begins with bringing the thought into the light. But once it is exposed, it has to be answered. The next question is whether that thought agrees with the truth of God's Word.

When he lies, he speaks his native language,
for he is a liar and the father of lies.

John 8:44

CHAPTER 5

Lies, Truth, and Obedience

Every thought we think is shaped by a voice. Sometimes it's our own inner voice. Sometimes it's the echo of someone else's words from the past. And sometimes it's the enemy himself, whispering lies. Jesus said that Satan "does not stand in the truth, because there is no truth in him… he is a liar and the father of lies" (John 8:44).

Lies and Partial Truths

From the beginning, Satan has twisted truth to stir doubt about God's goodness. In the garden, he planted the question, "Did God really say...?" He still works that way now, whispering lies that target our fear, shame, and longing. His lies may be subtle, but they are always aimed at the same target: pulling us away from trusting God.

He usually doesn't begin with an outright lie. More often, he takes a partial truth and isolates it. That's what makes partial truths so dangerous. They sound right at first because part of them is right, but they stop short of the whole truth. The enemy wants you to put a period where God puts a comma.

When we read, "apart from Me you can do nothing" (John 15:5), and stop there, we forget that abiding in Christ changes everything. We confess weakness and camp there, instead of continuing, "I can do all things through Christ who strengthens me" (Philippians 4:13). We admit, rightly, that we aren't worthy in and of ourselves. But then the enemy twists that into, *So God could never really love me, use me, or welcome me.* That's where a partial truth becomes a lie. Scripture says we've all sinned and fall short of the glory of God (Romans 3:23), but it also says that while we were still sinners, Christ died for us (Romans 5:8). On our own, we aren't worthy. But in Christ, we are loved, forgiven, and welcomed. That's how partial truths work. They stop short of the fullness of what God has said.

That same pattern shows up in the lies we tell ourselves. A woman feels rejected, and before long the thought becomes, *No one wants me.* A man fails at something, and the thought becomes, *I'll never get this right.* The heart latches onto those lies and dresses them up as truth. They sound convincing because they're fueled by emotion: *I feel abandoned, so I must be abandoned. I feel worthless, so I must be worthless. I feel hopeless, so there must be no hope.* But feelings don't determine what's true. Left unchecked, those lies can become strongholds. God has given us His Word. Scripture is not meant to merely inspire us; it judges the thoughts and attitudes of the heart (Hebrews 4:12). It cuts through the fog of emotion and exposes what is true.

When thoughts go unexamined and beliefs go unchallenged, those lies don't stay small. Over time, they begin shaping the way we think until we slowly conform to the pattern of this world rather than being renewed by God's truth (Romans 12:2). James goes further: "Friendship with the world means enmity against God" (James 4:4). This isn't a neutral drift. It's opposition. And the stakes aren't small. "The mind governed by the flesh is death, but the mind governed by the Spirit is life and peace" (Romans 8:6). One path numbs and deceives. The other leads to life.

Fruit is Evidence

The work doesn't stop at writing. Truth has to move from the page to the heart, and from the heart into the way we live. Belief always shows up in action. If we really believe what God says, our lives will reflect it.

Maybe that's part of why Psalm 34:8 says, "*Taste* and see that the Lord is good," instead of simply saying, "*Look* and see." We can look at something from a distance. Tasting requires up-close participation. You have to take something in. You have to personally receive it. In that sense, tasting fits obedience. Many people want to stand back and evaluate God's Word from a distance, doubting whether it's really true, whether it can really be trusted, whether God will really be faithful. But some things can only be known on the path of obedience. You taste and see when you trust Him enough to take Him at His Word and act on it. This isn't about earning God's goodness through obedience, but about coming to know it more deeply as you walk in it.

There's a misconception among some believers that fruit should appear automatically simply because they call themselves Christians. But fruit isn't automatic. It's the result of abiding obedience.

Paul writes, "The fruit of the Spirit is love, joy, peace, patience, kindness, goodness, faithfulness, gentleness, and self-control" (Galatians 5:22–23). Notice he calls it the fruit of the Spirit—not the fruit of feelings, and not the fruit of human effort. It comes from remaining in Christ. Jesus made that clear when He said, "I am the vine; you are the branches. If you remain in me and I in you, you will bear much fruit; apart from me you can do nothing" (John 15:5). Remaining in Him means obeying. It means not just hearing His Word, but doing what it says. James warns, "Do not merely listen to the word, and so deceive yourselves. Do what it says" (James 1:22).

When believers lack peace, joy, or patience, we should at least be willing to search our hearts for areas of disobedience. Too often, we blame our circumstances or start wondering why God seems to be holding out on us. But Scripture warns that sin disrupts fellowship with God: "Your iniquities have separated you from your God; your sins have hidden his face from you" (Isaiah 59:2). Fruitlessness is not because God withholds His Spirit, but because we resist Him through disobedience.

Abiding in Him isn't passive. It requires active obedience. Expecting fruit without obedience is like expecting a harvest without planting or watering seed. Paul exhorts believers,

"Since we live by the Spirit, let us keep in step with the Spirit" (Galatians 5:25). Fruit grows where faith is acted on.

Obedience is often dismissed as legalism. But legalism tries to earn God's love; obedience responds to it. Obedience isn't an ugly word. It's the evidence of love. Jesus said, "If you love me, keep my commands" (John 14:15). The Spirit produces fruit in those who abide in Christ through obedience. Neglect obedience, and fruit withers.

In other words, fruit isn't optional. It's the visible evidence of true discipleship.

Lies bend us inward toward fear, shame, and self-reliance. Truth lifts our eyes to Christ. And when truth moves from thought to action, we begin to live in the freedom He promised, bearing fruit that shows we belong to Him.

Let us examine our ways and test them,

and let us return to the Lord.

Lamentations 3:40

How to Use the Journal

Taking thoughts captive doesn't happen by accident. It takes practice. That's what Check Engine Light Journaling is designed to do. It's not about filling pages with ink. It's about learning to slow down, recognize the warning lights, and respond with truth and obedience.

When should you use the journal? Whenever you're experiencing an intense negative emotion. In this instance, we want our emotions to lead us, but only to the journal page—and from there, to the throne of God.

The Step-by-Step Process

If you don't want to use the companion Check Engine Light Journal, you can easily make your own with lined notebook paper. Leave the top of the page blank for the emotion, then draw a line straight down the center of the page. The left side will be for your thoughts. The right side will be for Scripture.

Step 1: Name the Emotion

At the very top of the page, in that blank space, write down the one-word emotion you're feeling—mad, sad, scared, anxious, lonely. Don't overthink it. The Psalms model this for us. David often begins his prayers with honesty: For example, he wrote, "Why, my soul, are you downcast? Why so disturbed within me?" (Psalm 42:5). He put words to his inner state–"downcast, disturbed." Naming the emotion gives you a clear starting point.

Step 2: What was happening?

Beneath that emotion word, write a sentence or two about what was happening just before you started to feel it. This helps you recognize patterns and become more aware of triggers. It's okay if nothing obvious comes to mind. But sometimes you'll notice a pattern—for example, that your anger spikes every time you get off the phone with your mother.

Step 3: Brain Dump

On the left-hand side of the page, write down every thought that comes to mind related to the emotion at the top of the page. Leave a line or two between thoughts, because you may need to rewrite or expand one later. Don't worry about putting the thoughts in order or making them sound reasonable. Just get them out where you can see them. Keep writing until you run out of steam. You may find you start repeating yourself, or start thinking about your grocery list… when that happens, you're done.

Don't censor yourself. Even if it sounds childish, shameful, or sinful, write it down. Most people don't struggle to identify their thoughts; they struggle to admit them. But if it's in there, it's shaping your emotions, and it needs to be brought into the light. As Jesus said, "For everyone who does evil hates the light, and will not come into the light for fear that their deeds will be exposed. But whoever lives by the truth comes into the light…" (John 3:20–21).

Step 4—Rewrite Questions as Statements:

If one of your thoughts is written as a question, rewrite it underneath the question as a statement. This is the purpose for leaving space between brain-dumped thoughts. Questions feel safer than statements, less exposed, less condemning.

For example, if you write, "What if I never change?" rewrite beneath it as, "I will never change." If you write, "What if no one really cares?" rewrite it as, "No one really cares."

This often feels uncomfortable, but that's the point. The statement is much more daunting and uglier than the question. Writing the thought as a statement exposes what you're actually believing. You're usually not just asking a question. Deep down, you've already answered it with the outcome you fear most.

Step 5: Identify the Hot Thought

A "hot thought" is the belief that carries the strongest emotional charge. Go back and read through what you've written. Which ones sting the most? Which ones make your stomach drop or your chest tighten? Which one brings tears to your eyes? These are the thoughts that need deeper digging.

Step 6: Dig Up the Roots

Now ask questions to get beneath the hot thought. Ask yourself: "So what?"—Meaning—"So what if this is true?" "What does it mean if it's true?" "What does it say about me if it's true?" "What's the worst that could happen if it's true?" and "Why would that be so terrible?" Write down those root fears and beliefs. Often you'll find that the surface thought ("I can't face this") connects to a deeper lie ("I'm alone," "God won't help me," "No one cares about me"). After you've traced the roots, circle the one that hits hardest—that's your true hot thought.

Step 7: Truth in Scripture

Now turn to the right-hand side of the page. This is where you fight lies with truth. Write down Scripture that speaks directly to the thought or root fear. Don't paraphrase it. Write the verse out word for word, along with the reference.

If you don't know where to find a verse, don't panic. Open Google and type, "What does the Bible say about _______?" Fill in the blank with your thought or fear. If you type, "What does the Bible say about abandonment?" you'll likely find several verses. Read through them and choose the one that speaks most directly to the ache in your heart. That's the one to write down. Over time, you'll start to memorize verses, and the Spirit will bring them to mind when you need them.

Step 8: The Call to Action

Faith doesn't stop at writing down truth, it acts on it. At the bottom of the page, write at least three actions you'll take to live like you believe the Scripture you wrote.

If God's Word says He is with you, what step will you take today that shows you believe He hasn't abandoned you? If His Word says you're forgiven, what step will you take that shows you're living forgiven instead of condemned? If His Word says He is faithful, what step will you take that shows you trust Him with what you can't control? Maybe that means making the phone call you've been avoiding, having the hard conversation you've been putting off, or going to church and choosing to pray instead of isolating and spiraling.

If that feels hard to answer, picture someone who truly believed this verse. How would they act right now? Sometimes we're too tangled up in our own thoughts to see the next obedient step clearly. Imagining someone else living out the verse can force us outside our own head long enough to recognize where obedience is needed.

For example:

If your lie says, "I'm abandoned," and the Scripture says, "I will never leave you nor forsake you" (Hebrews 13:5), your actions might be:

- Pray out loud, thanking God for His presence.
- Call a trusted Christian friend instead of isolating.
- Read Psalm 23 every morning this week.

If your lie says, "I can't handle this" and the Scripture says, "God is our refuge and strength, an ever-present help in trouble" (Psalm 46:1), your actions might be:

- Walk into the situation you've been avoiding instead of running from it.
- Pray before you respond instead of spiraling.
- Do the next obedient thing in front of you, even if you still feel afraid.

If your lie says, "I've ruined everything" and the Scripture says, "There is now no condemnation for those who are in Christ Jesus" (Romans 8:1), your actions might be:

- Confess your sin without hiding or minimizing.
- Speak honestly to the person you wronged instead of withdrawing in shame.
- Thank God for His mercy instead of rehearsing self-condemnation.

If your lie says, "I have every right to explode" and the Scripture says, "Everyone should be quick to listen, slow to speak and slow to become angry" (James 1:19), your actions might be:

- Lower your voice instead of raising it.
- Leave the room long enough to pray before responding.

- Go back and answer gently instead of lashing out.

When You Face Resistance

You can expect to face resistance in this process. If you struggle to find a verse, don't assume God is hiding His truth from you. Ask, seek, and keep looking.

Other times, you may finish writing and feel no emotional shift at all. Don't get discouraged. Feelings often lag behind obedience. Thoughts and actions often move long before feelings do. You're not chasing emotional relief; you're practicing faithfulness. Trust what God has said, not what you feel in the moment.

You may also notice the same thought returning again and again. That doesn't mean the process is failing. Each time the thought resurfaces, capture it again. For those stubborn thoughts, consider writing the lie on one side of an index card and the corresponding Scripture on the other. Carry it with you and pull it out when the light comes on.

SAMPLE JOURNAL ENTRY

Anxious

<u>Preparing for a meeting at work.</u>

Brain Dump	God's Word
I'm going to fail.	The Lord is my helper; I will not be afraid. (Hebrews 13:6)
No one respects me.	My grace is sufficient for you. (2 Corinthians 12:9)
If I mess this up, it will all fall apart.	Cast your cares on the LORD and he will sustain you; he will never let the righteous be shaken. (Psalm 55:22)

Action Steps:

Speak calmly instead of withdrawing.

Pray Hebrews 13:6 before the meeting.

Maintain eye contact and trust God with the outcome.

*Do not conform to the pattern of this world,
but be transformed by the renewing of your
mind. Then you will be able to test and
approve what God's will is—his good,
pleasing and perfect will.*

Romans 12:2

Chapter 7

Renewal and Perseverance

Taking a thought captive is the moment of obedience. Renewing the mind is the long-term transformation that follows. Paul wrote, "Do not conform to the pattern of this world, but be transformed by the renewing of your mind" (Romans 12:2). That's the goal of this entire process. The Check Engine Light Journal isn't about venting emotions or chasing short-term relief. It's about lasting transformation. When we obey God's command to take every thought captive, we're training our minds to stop following lies and start following truth.

Information vs. Transformation

There's a difference between knowing Scripture and being changed by it. The Pharisees knew the Scriptures backward and forward, yet Jesus called them hypocrites because their hearts remained unchanged (Matthew 23:27–28). They had information, but not transformation.

Paul warned Timothy about people "having a form of godliness but denying its power" (2 Timothy 3:5). That's what happens when we treat the Word of God as head knowledge but never let it reshape our lives. Transformation comes when we do not merely read or memorize Scripture, but obey it.

Patterns of Thought

Old lies are like ruts in a dirt road. The more often you drive through them, the deeper they become. Your mind naturally falls back into them, even when you know they lead somewhere destructive. Rehearsed beliefs become easier to return to over time (Hebb, 1949; Doidge, 2007).

Without renewal, we keep falling back into the same lies—anger, fear, shame, self-condemnation—because those grooves feel familiar.

Renewal happens when truth is repeated and acted on often enough that a different path begins to form. Each time you confront a lie with truth and act on it, you're strengthening a new way of thinking. Over time, the old ruts begin to grow over, and the path shaped by truth becomes easier to walk. Just like exercise builds strength one rep at a time, renewal builds through daily obedience. "Train yourself to be godly" (1 Timothy 4:7).

The Role of the Spirit

We can't renew our minds by sheer willpower. Only the Holy Spirit can apply God's Word deeply enough to reshape us. Jesus promised that the Spirit would "teach you all things and remind you of everything I have said to you" (John 14:26). As you rehearse Scripture and act on it, the Spirit brings truth back to mind when you need it most. Renewal is His work. Journaling is simply one tool that helps you participate through obedience.

A Personal Example

There was a season in my life when it felt like the rug had been pulled out from under me. My entire world was shaken. I was devastated after discovering my husband's infidelity, and I felt more broken than I ever thought a person could feel.

I sought counseling from a godly older gentleman. But inside, I doubted he could help me. I remember thinking, *If he could see what I feel on the inside, he would rush me to the emergency room. I feel like I'm bleeding out.* What words could possibly reach me in that state?

We sat across the table from one another, and he quietly wrote something on a piece of paper. Then he slid it across to me. On it were these words:

"Faith is believing the Word of God and acting upon it, no matter how I feel, knowing He promises a good result."

He told me to memorize it and come back in a week. I didn't show it outwardly, but inside I was rolling my eyes. *How could memorizing this possibly help me?* Honestly, I was irritated. It felt too simple for the level of pain I was in. I wanted relief, not a sentence to memorize. I wanted someone to tell me how to survive what felt unsurvivable. Still, I went home and memorized it. (Back then I was more "type A" than I am now—God has since softened me a lot!)

Then one day, another wave of bad news hit me, and I collapsed under the weight of it. I was lying on the floor, in my pajamas, hadn't showered for days. I was such a mess that my young son had to get himself a Pop-Tart because I couldn't even pull myself together enough to make him food.

As I cried, he came down the stairs, looked at me, and said: "Mom, don't you think God is going to help us?"

That question cut straight through the fog. It was simple, childlike, and impossible to dodge. In that moment, I could see the gap between what I said I believed and how I was actually living.

It reminds me of a child playing outside while the parent watches through the window. The child falls, scrapes her knee, and runs crying toward the house. The parent already saw what happened. The parent knows what the child needs and is able to help—clean the wound, bandage the knee, comfort the child, and decide what needs to happen next. But if the child runs past the parent, shuts herself in her room, and refuses comfort, the issue isn't the parent's awareness, willingness, or ability. The issue is trust.

In the same way, God is never powerless to help us. Our resistance doesn't limit His ability. But when we run from Him, refuse His Word, or insist on our own way, we're not receiving His help in faith; we're resisting Him in pride. Scripture warns that "God opposes the proud but shows favor to the humble" (James 4:6). Humility runs to Him. Pride hides, argues, blames, or tries to manage the pain alone. That's why true faith cannot remain theoretical; if I believed His Word, I had to act on it.

My son's question brought conviction and exposed that same issue in me. I said I believed God would help us, but my actions were telling a different story.

Maybe this is part of what Jesus meant when He said we must become like little children (Matthew 18:3). Children trust. They believe what they're told, and they act on it. My son's question carried that kind of simple trust. He wasn't overanalyzing or filled with worry. He simply believed God would help us. In that moment, his childlike faith exposed how far I had drifted from that kind of trust. That was when what I had been memorizing finally clicked. Up until then, I had only repeated the words to prove to my counselor that I'd done my homework. But suddenly, they became alive in me. I thought: *I'm certainly not acting like someone who believes God is working all things together for her good, am I?*

So I got up. I made my son a peanut butter and jelly sandwich. I threw in a load of laundry and got into the shower. They may seem like small things, but for me, each one was an act of faith.

None of those things changed my circumstances. They didn't take the pain away. They were the first small acts of obedience I could take.

They were my way of saying, *If I really believe God is working all things for my good, then this is what someone who believes that would do.*

After about a week of acting on His Word rather than my feelings, I collapsed before the Lord. My circumstances hadn't changed, and every time I moved in the direction faith was calling me, my feelings still refused to budge. I started to feel like a fraud, a hypocrite. One evening I fell on my face before the Lord and cried out, "Father, You know me. You knit me together in my mother's womb. You know I'm a what-you-see-is-what-you-get kind of girl. I feel like I'm faking it. I don't think I can keep going like this."

And the Holy Spirit, quietly and gently, spoke to my heart: "It's called obedience."

You know it's the Lord when He says something you would never have told yourself in that moment, and when the truth of it cuts straight through you. My weeping came to a halt as I knelt there on the floor, almost stunned. *Could this be true? Is this what obedience looks like?*

Then I began to think about my son. That realization also changed the way I understood obedience as a parent.

He didn't always understand the things I asked him to do, and he certainly didn't always like them. But what did I want from him in those moments? Obedience. I wanted him to trust me because I'm wiser and because I love him. When he was a child, I knew what was best for him in ways he couldn't yet understand. I knew that one day, he'd be glad I made him brush his teeth and eat his vegetables. In that moment, I realized I'd been expecting obedience to feel like agreement. But sometimes obedience feels like surrender—doing what God says even when everything in you resists. I've also likened it to picking up one lead foot and throwing it out in front of the other.

That moment was the beginning of a turning point for me. I would never have chosen that season. At the time, it felt like devastation. But looking back, I can say something that once would've sounded impossible: I'm grateful for what God produced through it. The betrayal didn't destroy my faith; it refined it. I began to understand what it really means to count trials as joy—not because they feel good, but because of what God produces through them (James 1:2–4).

Christ alone was able to hold me up, comfort me, and love me in a way no human ever could. I had leaned on my husband—and he failed. I had leaned on friends—and they fell short. I had leaned on family and even the church—and they couldn't carry what I was asking them to carry. That's not cruelty; it's humanity. Every person will fail you at some point. Only Christ will not.

I came to know the Lord in that furnace in a way I never would have otherwise. You don't cling to Christ because you already know He's sufficient; you discover He's sufficient when He's all you have left. The trial was bitter. His presence in it was sweet. And through that fire, my faith became steadier, deeper, and more real than it had ever been.

Faith stopped being something I said I had or words on the pages of the Bible and started becoming action in my life.

That "Faith is" statement became a two-way lens for me. It helped me look inward at my own heart and outward at my circumstances. I'd encourage you to memorize it and use it the same way. Hold it up to yourself and ask, "If this is true, how should I be acting right now?" Then hold it up to your situation and ask, "If God promises a good result, what might He be doing that I can't yet see?"

The Fruit of a Renewed Mind

A renewed mind bears fruit. Peace begins to replace anxiety, just as Scripture promises that "the peace of God, which transcends all understanding, will guard your hearts and your minds in Christ Jesus" (Philippians 4:7). Joy begins to grow even in suffering, because we learn to "consider it pure joy knowing that the testing of your faith produces perseverance" (James 1:2–3). Hope begins to shine through despair as "the God of hope" fills us "with all joy and peace in believing" so that we may abound in hope by the power of the Holy Spirit (Romans 15:13).

When Growth Feels Slow

One of the hardest parts of the Christian life is how slowly growth often happens. We live in a culture of quick fixes and instant results, but sanctification doesn't move at that pace. Patterns formed over years don't disappear in days. They resurface, sometimes with surprising force. That doesn't mean you've failed. It means you're still in the process. Paul compared spiritual growth to planting and harvest: "Let us not grow weary in doing good, for at the proper time we will reap a harvest if we do not give up" (Galatians 6:9).

Hebrews 11 gives us example after example of this kind of faith. Abraham left home without knowing where he was going. Moses confronted Pharaoh. Noah built an ark before there was rain. The emphasis isn't on how they felt, but on the fact that they obeyed. Faith has always meant acting on what God has said, even in the face of uncertainty, fear, or incomplete understanding.

Dry Seasons

There will also be days, or even weeks, when journaling feels mechanical. You may write the words and feel nothing. You may wonder, Is this even working? In those moments, it's easy to give up. Feelings aren't the measure of obedience. Faithfulness is. When you keep writing, keep searching the Scriptures, and keep acting on them, you're sowing seeds that will bear fruit in due time. Even if your journal entry feels repetitive, write it anyway. Obedience is never wasted.

God's Faithfulness in the Process

The good news is that perseverance isn't just about your strength to keep going. God Himself sustains you. Paul reminded the Philippians, "He who began a good work in you will carry it on to completion until the day of Christ Jesus" (Philippians 1:6).

Even when you feel weak, God is still at work within you. "It is God who works in you to will and to act in order to fulfill his good purpose" (Philippians 2:13). That means perseverance is less about gritting your teeth and more about leaning on His grace day by day. Look back from time to time and reread old entries. You'll often see growth you didn't notice in the moment.

The Reward of Endurance

Hebrews calls us to "run with endurance the race marked out for us, fixing our eyes on Jesus, the pioneer and perfecter of faith" (Hebrews 12:1–2). Faith isn't a sprint. It's a marathon. Renewal of the mind and transformation of the heart don't happen in one journal entry or even one season of journaling. They require perseverance.

Scripture is clear that perseverance carries great reward. James wrote, "Blessed is the one who perseveres under trial because, having stood the test, that person will receive the crown of life that the Lord has promised to those who love him" (James 1:12). Paul reminded us that suffering produces endurance, and endurance produces character, and character produces hope (Romans 5:3–4).

Perseverance isn't glamorous. It's often quiet, unseen, and difficult. But it's through perseverance that the Spirit matures us, hope takes root, and fruit begins to show.

So when you're tempted to quit—when the journal feels heavy, when the lies feel louder than the truth—remember this: you're in a race marked out by God Himself. Keep your eyes on Jesus. Keep writing. Keep obeying. He is faithful, and He will bring you to the finish line.

At the end of his own race, Paul was able to say, "I have fought the good fight, I have finished the race, I have kept the faith" (2 Timothy 4:7). That's the goal of perseverance. When the check engine light comes on, perseverance means responding to it rightly and continuing the race.

Encouragement

The pace of renewal may feel slow, but God works according to an appointed time. Even when it seems delayed, He's not late (Habakkuk 2:3). So don't despise the small steps. Every page, every verse, and every act of obedience matters more than you can see in the moment. God is at work, even when the change feels quiet and slow.

But this perseverance isn't merely psychological discipline. Scripture describes it as a battle. God has not left believers defenseless. He's given them armor.

PART THREE:

Armor and Community

Therefore put on the full armor of God, so that when the day of evil comes, you may be able to stand your ground, and after you have done everything, to stand.

Ephesians 6:13

CHAPTER 8

The Armor and the Sword

Paul wrote to the Ephesians, "Be strong in the Lord and in his mighty power. Put on the full armor of God, so that you can take your stand against the devil's schemes" (Ephesians 6:10–11). The Christian life isn't lived on neutral ground. We are in a battle, and our enemy is relentless. But God has not left us exposed—He has given us armor.

The Belt of Truth

A soldier's belt wasn't an accessory; it held everything else together. In the same way, truth is what holds our lives in place. Lies loosen everything. The journaling process is one way of fastening on the belt of truth. It helps us expose lies and anchor ourselves in what God has said.

Without truth, nothing else in the armor will stay secure. That's what's happening when someone gets one disappointing text, one awkward look, or one hard conversation and immediately starts building a whole false story around it. Truth stops the spiral before it pulls everything else out of place.

The Breastplate of Righteousness

The breastplate protected the soldier's vital organs, especially the heart. Our righteousness doesn't come from ourselves but from Christ. When the enemy accuses—"You're a failure. You're unworthy. You'll never measure up"—we stand protected, not in our own goodness, but in His. That matters when a believer keeps replaying yesterday's failure and starts relating to God as though Christ's righteousness no longer covers them.

The enemy often accuses with facts. Yes, you've sinned. Yes, you fall short. But accusation isn't the whole story. The gospel doesn't leave you exposed in your failure. "There is now no condemnation for those who are in Christ Jesus" (Romans 8:1). In Christ, the guilty are forgiven, the lost are found, and the unworthy are made righteous.

The Shield of Faith

Roman shields were large, often covering the whole body. Soldiers could extinguish fiery arrows by soaking their shields in water before battle. Paul says faith is our shield: "Take up the shield of faith, with which you can extinguish all the flaming arrows of the evil one" (Ephesians 6:16). Lies and emotions often come like fiery darts—sudden, hot, burning. Faith raises the shield by saying, "I will believe what God has said over what I feel right now." Faith is not merely agreeing with truth; it's acting on it.

Sometimes that looks like obeying while fear is still screaming, choosing not to fire back in anger, or moving forward without demanding that your feelings line up first.

The Helmet of Salvation

The helmet guards the head—the place of thoughts, decisions, and identity. Salvation covers us with the assurance of who we are in Christ. Without that assurance, every lie can strike the mind. But with it, we can say, "I belong to Jesus. My eternity is secure. My mind is guarded by His promise." The helmet of salvation reminds us of our position in Christ, not just our condition in the moment.

When shame tries to define you by your worst moment, the helmet of salvation reminds you that your identity was settled at the cross.

Standing Firm

Paul repeats the command "stand" multiple times in Ephesians 6. Lies try to knock us off balance. Emotions try to sweep us away. But with truth, righteousness, faith, and salvation, we can stand firm—protected by the armor God provides.

But armor alone isn't enough. God also gives us a weapon.

The Sword of the Spirit

When Paul lists the armor of God in Ephesians 6, nearly every piece is defensive. The belt, the breastplate, the shield, the helmet—they guard and protect. But then he names one weapon designed not merely to withstand attack, but to strike: "Take the helmet of salvation and the sword of the Spirit, which is the word of God" (Ephesians 6:17). The Word of God isn't passive, nor is it sentimental inspiration for hard seasons. It's a weapon.

Hebrews tells us, "For the word of God is alive and active. Sharper than any double-edged sword, it penetrates even to dividing soul and spirit, joints and marrow; it judges the thoughts and attitudes of the heart" (Hebrews 4:12). The Word cuts, exposes, and separates truth from deception. When Jesus was tempted in the wilderness, He didn't debate Satan. He didn't appeal to emotion. He didn't rely on logic alone. He answered every temptation with the same phrase: "It is written" (Matthew 4:4, 7, 10). The sword was sufficient.

The sword of the Spirit was not given as decoration or mere display, but to be used—believed and obeyed. That is what Check Engine Light Journaling trains you to do. You're not merely coping. You're cutting down falsehood with truth. Every time you choose to believe what God has said over what you feel, you swing the blade.

A Lamp for the Path

Scripture also gives us another image of the Word: "Your word is a lamp to my feet and a light to my path" (Psalm 119:105). In ancient times, a lamp wasn't a spotlight. It was a small clay vessel filled with oil and fitted with a wick. When lit, it didn't flood the landscape with light. It illuminated only a few steps ahead.

Let's face it, we want floodlights. We want clarity about next year, next month, the final outcome. God gives a lamp. He lights the next step. Faith isn't walking with full visibility. It's walking with sufficient light for obedience. If you refuse to move until you can see the whole road, you'll stand still in the dark. If you trust the lamp, you move forward one step at a time.

Daily Bread and Dependence

But a lamp only helps if it is kept lit. In the same way, the Word can't guide a life that neglects it. Jesus said, "Man shall not live on bread alone, but on every word that comes from the mouth of God" (Matthew 4:4). Bread sustains physical life. The Word sustains spiritual life. Daily bread isn't a metaphor for occasional inspiration. It's a picture of dependence.

Jesus declared, "I am the bread of life" (John 6:35) and offered living water that satisfies forever (John 4:14). When He spoke of eating His flesh and drinking His blood, He was calling people to total dependence on Him—to receive Him fully by faith, to trust in His sacrifice, to live by His life. We don't consume Scripture as a ritual. We feed on Christ by faith, and we encounter Him through His Word. To neglect the Word is to neglect the very means by which we know the One who saves us.

I liken the Word of God to "brain floss." It clears out the buildup we don't even realize is there. And just like our teeth, neglect is enough to cause decay. You don't have to deliberately sabotage your mind to drift into deception. You only have to leave it unattended. Most of us understand the importance of brushing our teeth every day. How much more important, then, is the regular intake of the Word of God for the spiritual health of our minds and hearts? When the Word is neglected, we don't simply lose information. We lose light.

Two Ditches on the Road

Without a lamp, you don't just hesitate—you misstep, running into obstacles you could've avoided and falling into ditches you never saw coming. In the dark, you don't only end up hurting yourself; you collide with other people and wound them too. Decisions made without light rarely stay small; they grow into consequences we never intended. In time, that darkness bears rotten fruit.

There are two ditches on this road. One is paralysis. We refuse to move because we can't see far enough ahead. Fear convinces us that waiting for certainty is wisdom, so we stand still and call it caution. It looks like the woman who lies awake night after night, replaying the same decision, telling herself she will move once she feels peace, while obedience keeps getting pushed farther down the road. The other ditch is haste. We move quickly without light, driven by impulse or emotion, and then wonder why we're bruised and bleeding. It looks like the husband who feels hurt, fires off cutting words in the heat of the moment, and only later sees the damage he has done. One refuses to step. The other runs blindly. Both abandon the lamp.

Some believers get stuck in the paralysis ditch and call it "waiting on wisdom." Scripture says, "If any of you lacks wisdom, you should ask God… and it will be given to you" (James 1:5). It doesn't say wait for a light bulb moment. It doesn't say wait for a sign or a surge of peace. It says ask—and it will be given. Wisdom isn't a feeling. Biblically, wisdom is skill in godly living. It's the God-given ability to choose the most obedient option in front of you and move forward in trust.

I've heard people say, "I knew it was right because I felt peace." But peace isn't the test of obedience. If we only did what felt peaceful, we would rarely obey. Jesus said, "Love your enemies" (Matthew 5:44). No one wakes up feeling eager to do that. Faith and feelings often stand at a fork in the road. Wisdom doesn't wait for feelings to cooperate. It chooses obedience and moves even when feelings contradict.

When we stop opening the Bible, we don't just stay where we are. We drift. Slowly. Quietly. Our emotions begin to lead us instead of inform us. Fear starts making decisions for us. Anger gets louder than wisdom. Shame convinces us to withdraw. And we listen, because we've forgotten what God actually said. The drift doesn't feel dramatic. It feels normal. That's what makes it dangerous. We move through situations convinced our feelings are reliable guides, yet unsure of what's actually true. And then we're surprised by the consequences. The problem isn't the intensity of the emotion. It's that we stopped letting God's Word light the way.

The armor protects. The sword strikes. Together, they equip us to stand firm in a battle that wages not just around us, but within us—in the thoughts we think and the lies we're tempted to believe. The Word of God isn't only a lamp for our steps; it is the blade that cuts through deception. Without it, we stumble and are exposed. With it, lies are confronted and our path is made clear. This is how the believer stands—not by emotion, sight, or any other sense, but by faith in the truth God has spoken. We walk by faith, not by sight (2 Corinthians 5:7).

I pour out before Him my complaint;

before Him I tell my trouble.

Psalm 142:2

Chapter 9

Fervent Prayer and Lament

James writes, "The effectual fervent prayer of a righteous man availeth much" (James 5:16, KJV). The word 'fervent' carries the sense of intensity and earnestness—not detached or restrained, but deeply engaged, even at the level of strong emotion. Scripture doesn't condemn intense emotion; it gives it a destination. Our strongest emotions were never meant to be self-contained or independently managed. They were fashioned with direction in mind. They were meant to be carried into the presence of the One who formed us and brought under His authority.

Paul likewise commands believers to "pray in the Spirit on all occasions" (Ephesians 6:18), reminding us that true prayer isn't an emotional impulse untethered from truth. It's Spirit-dependent, aligned with God's will, and anchored in obedience. Biblical fervency isn't chaos but intensity directed under God's authority.

Scripture gives this kind of prayer a name: lament. "I pour out before Him my complaint; before Him I tell my trouble" (Psalm 142:2). "How long, O Lord? Will you forget me forever?" (Psalm 13:1). Many of the Psalms are laments—raw, unfiltered sorrow directed not away from God but toward Him. God's Word doesn't hide the grief of His people; it records it. Lament isn't grumbling about God; it's grief brought to God. Israel grumbled in the wilderness and hardened their hearts against God. David lamented and remained in relationship. The difference is direction.

When emotion surges, it often feels chaotic and loud. Anger comes crashing and grief floods. Fear can paralyze us. It feels like wind and waves with no restraint. But chaos doesn't mean something is wrong with God's design. It means we're trying to hold something we were never meant to hold alone.

Hannah wept bitterly before the Lord (1 Samuel 1:10). Her prayer was so intense that Eli assumed she was drunk. But she wasn't unraveling; she was pouring herself out before God. Hezekiah received a threatening letter and "spread it before the

Lord" (2 Kings 19:14). He didn't first strategize or collapse into panic; he laid the weight of it before God. Even Jesus in Gethsemane said, "My soul is overwhelmed with sorrow to the point of death" (Matthew 26:38), and being in anguish, He prayed more earnestly (Luke 22:44). The intensity of His emotions wasn't suppressed; it was directed.

Anger, grief, fear, desperation—these aren't defects. They're forces God uses to drive us to Himself. They expose what we believe and reveal where we're still clinging to control. They press us toward dependence. Negative emotions aren't meant to be eliminated; they're meant to grow our relationship with Him. They're signals that something in you needs to be brought before the Lord. When we try to contain it ourselves or discharge it onto other people, we short-circuit its design. But when we bring it to Him, what feels chaotic comes under His authority. The storm may still rage, but it no longer rules.

Our emotions were made to move us toward the Creator, not away from Him. They're designed to drive us into dependence on the only One who speaks to wind and waves and is obeyed. Through that dependence, He reshapes us. What we often experience as turmoil becomes one of His primary instruments of sanctification. And when the storm quiets in His presence, we're finally able to hear Him clearly enough to obey faithfully. Like Jeremiah in the middle of devastation who declared, "Great is Your faithfulness" (Lamentations 3:23), lament doesn't deny sorrow; it anchors it in truth.

When the light is blinking, most of us run for relief before we run to God. We medicate it, distract it, intellectualize it, socialize it. We call someone. We scroll. We vent. By the time we pray, the heat has cooled and the urgency has thinned. But God invites us to bring the full intensity to Him. "Pour out your hearts to Him, for God is our refuge" (Psalm 62:8). He isn't asking for edited emotion. He's asking for fervent prayer poured out before Him. Scripture not only commands this kind of prayer; it shows us how to do it.

Out, In, Up

Here's how we can respond when the dashboard lights up:

First: Out

Pour out the full weight of your emotion before God. Don't sanitize it or censor it because it doesn't yet sound spiritual. The Psalms don't begin with polished theology; they begin with honesty. "My tears have been my food day and night" (Psalm 42:3). "Why have You forgotten me?" (Psalm 42:9). God invites that kind of honesty: "Pour out your heart before

Him; God is a refuge for us" (Psalm 62:8). This isn't irreverence; it's relationship with God. Lament brings the raw heart before God rather than hiding it from Him. The honesty isn't the final word, but it is the beginning. I did this when I finally fell on my face before the Lord and told Him the truth: "I feel like I'm faking it."

Communicating with God—that's all prayer really is. We don't need to be cleaned up first. If we did, we'd never come, and we wouldn't need God. We don't need special words or rehearsed verses. We need to be real and raw before Him. And if you can't think of any words, that's okay too. Sometimes all we can do is cry, but let your cry be directed toward Him.

Paul tells us, "the Spirit helps us in our weakness. We do not know what we ought to pray for, but the Spirit Himself intercedes for us through wordless groans" (Romans 8:26). Sometimes the only words we can muster are, "God, help me." Our prayers can feel like a tangled mess when our emotions are raw. But what feels jumbled and inarticulate to us is not presented to the Father that way. The Spirit takes our broken cry and intercedes according to the will of God. We often think we've brought our emotion to God, only to rush away before we've truly poured it out.

Remain there and let the wind rage in His presence. The circumstances may not immediately change. The hurt may not disappear. But the volume shifts. The panic subsides. The chaos quiets enough for you to hear Him. And when you can hear Him, you can obey.

Second: In

After pouring out what is true about your heart, bring in what is true about God. David does this repeatedly: "Why, my soul, are you downcast? … Put your hope in God" (Psalm 42:5). This is where truth confronts distortion. The lie says, "I'm alone." The Word says, "I will never leave you nor forsake you" (Hebrews 13:5). The emotion says, "This will destroy me." The Word says, "My grace is sufficient for you" (2 Corinthians 12:9). This isn't denial of feeling; it's correction of interpretation. In my own prayer, I had to remind myself that God made me, knew me, and was not confused by what I was feeling.

Finally: Up

Then rise from your knees and *act* as though God's Word is more reliable than what you feel. Jesus didn't leave Gethsemane still debating. He rose and walked toward the cross. "Not my will, but Yours be done" (Luke 22:42) was not poetic language; it was obedient action. James reminds us to be doers of the word, not hearers only (James 1:22). Fervent prayer doesn't end on the floor. It stands up in faith. For me, that looked like getting up, making my son a sandwich, throwing in a load of laundry, and doing the next obedient thing in front of me. Those ordinary acts weren't glamorous, but they were faith getting up off the floor. That's where fervent prayer leads—not merely to relief, but to surrendered obedience.

Therefore confess your sins to each other and pray for each other so that you may be healed. The prayer of a righteous person is powerful and effective.

James 5:16

Chapter 10

Community and Confession

The Christian life was never meant to be lived alone. From the beginning, God declared, "It is not good for man to be alone" (Genesis 2:18). He created us for fellowship with one another. That design doesn't change in the battle for our thoughts and emotions.

The body of Christ is essential—but it's not the Head. Support is a gift, not a substitute. We weren't built to serve as one another's final refuge. Go to God first. Stay there. Let Him steady you. Then invite the body to stand with you.

James writes, "Therefore confess your sins to each other and pray for each other so that you may be healed. The effectual fervent prayer of a righteous man availeth much" (James 5:16,

KJV). Notice what is tied together: confession, prayer, and healing.

Wounds rarely heal in secrecy. Confession isn't emotional dumping, nor is it venting for relief. First and foremost, confession is made before God, who is "faithful and just to forgive us our sins and to cleanse us from all unrighteousness" (1 John 1:9). He doesn't merely hear confession; He forgives and washes clean. But Scripture also calls us to bring sin and struggle into the light with trusted believers.

Confession is humble agreement with God about sin, weakness, and misplaced belief. When confession follows fervent prayer, it's no longer chaotic; it's purposeful. We're not asking others to carry what only God can bear. We're inviting them to stand with us under His authority.

I've seen this difference in counseling. One person calls three friends just to unload and feel lighter for the moment, but nothing actually changes. Another person confesses, "I've been believing a lie, I've been feeding my anger, and I need prayer and accountability to respond differently." One is venting for relief. The other is inviting someone into obedience. The first seeks emotional discharge. The second seeks spiritual strengthening.

God has designed confession to break secrecy. Lies, like fungus, grow when kept in the dark. When we confess, we expose what shame tries to protect. We drag hidden thoughts into the light and allow the body of Christ to pray, exhort, and restore.

The healing James describes doesn't always mean immediate physical relief. It includes spiritual restoration, relational repair, and renewed obedience. God often uses the prayers of other believers as part of that healing process.

Bearing Burdens Together

Paul instructs us, "Carry each other's burdens, and in this way you will fulfill the law of Christ" (Galatians 6:2). To bear one another's burdens doesn't mean replacing God as refuge. It means reinforcing one another in obedience. It means reminding each other of truth when emotions threaten to drown it out.

Scripture also commends the wisdom of seeking counsel. "For lack of guidance a nation falls, but victory is won through many advisers" (Proverbs 11:14). And again, "Plans fail for lack of counsel, but with many advisers they succeed" (Proverbs 15:22). Seeking godly counsel isn't weakness; it's wisdom. But counsel functions rightly only when it flows from submission to God, not substitution for Him.

There's danger when the order is reversed. When we instinctively run to people before we run to God, we place weight on them they were never meant to hold. Even good gifts can become idols when they become the first place we run. Friends, mentors, pastors, therapists—these are gifts of grace. But they're not the Head. Christ is the Head of the body (Colossians 1:18). The body functions properly only when it remains connected to Him. God often brings healing through the prayers, truth, and presence of His people.

Practical Ways to Live This Out

Living in biblical community requires intention; it doesn't happen accidentally. Practicing that intentionality begins with wisdom about how and with whom we share. Share selectively. Not every journal page needs to be public, but when a lie feels especially strong, invite a trusted believer into the struggle. Pray together. Ask someone to pray the Scripture you wrote in your journal. Hearing truth spoken aloud strengthens faith. Seek accountability by inviting someone to follow up on the actions you committed to take. Stay connected. Make fellowship a rhythm, not an emergency measure. Growth is steadier in consistent community.

The enemy prefers isolation. Shame isolates. But Ecclesiastes reminds us, "Though one may be overpowered, two can defend themselves. A cord of three strands is not quickly broken" (Ecclesiastes 4:12).

Community isn't the first refuge. It's the supporting structure. God designed us for dependence on Him and interdependence with one another. In that order, healing becomes possible, perseverance is strengthened, and the battle isn't fought alone.

He heals the brokenhearted and

binds up their wounds.

Psalm 147:3

Conclusion

When the Light Comes On Again

By now, you know this truth: your emotions are not the problem. They're signals—God-designed indicators that something beneath the surface needs attention. They're not meant to be ignored, silenced, or numbed, but brought before God.

For much of our lives, many of us have been taught to fear painful emotions—to escape them, numb them, explain them away, or manage them just enough to function. But God offers us something far better than management. He uses even painful emotions as a tool in our sanctification, drawing us to Himself. And as we draw near to Him, He draws near to us (James 4:8).

This process trains us to do one thing: respond rightly when the light comes on. Check Engine Light Journaling provides a framework: bring the emotion to God, confront the lie with truth, and walk in obedience. Sometimes obedience will bring relief quickly. Other times it won't. But it always leads to life, and the fruit of the Spirit grows from it.

This process works not because it's clever, but because it aligns with how God designed the human heart and mind to function. Human systems may observe the pattern, but only God can heal and transform. When emotions flare, they get our attention. When we slow down and write, we expose what the heart is believing. When we bring those beliefs under the authority of Scripture, truth confronts lies. Light begins to shine in those dark spaces. And when we act on that truth—whether we feel like it or not—faith becomes visible. As James says, "I will show you my faith by my deeds" (James 2:18).

You won't always feel calm, brave, or confident when you take the next step God calls you to take. Faith doesn't wait for emotions to cooperate. It moves forward in obedience, trusting God with the outcome.

There will be days when this journal feels repetitive. Days when the same lies resurface. Days when the emotions feel louder than the truth. That doesn't mean the process is failing. It means sanctification is still at work. Growth is often quiet, slow, and unseen—like roots forming beneath the soil. Obedience is the nourishment God uses to deepen them.

Scripture says, "Foolishness is bound up in the heart of a child" (Proverbs 22:15). So when Jesus calls us to become like little children, He isn't praising childish foolishness. He's commending childlike trust. Remember who you are in this relationship. You're not the parent holding everything together. You're the child. A small child doesn't stop and formulate a five-step plan when they're hurt. A child runs crying to the one they trust, bringing their tears, pain, and confusion. That's the posture God calls us to—not self-sufficiency or polished strength, but childlike dependence. Don't run past Him and shut the door. Don't be the foolish child who keeps trying to bandage her own wounds when her Father is standing right there with open arms. Bring it all to Him. The question isn't whether He can sustain you. The question is whether you believe He will.

Some things can only be known on the path of obedience. You don't taste and see by sitting on the sidelines. You taste and see when you trust Him enough to take Him at His Word and act on it. Growth usually doesn't happen in dramatic leaps. It happens in the next small act of obedience. You don't have to conquer everything today. Just bring Him the next emotion, confront the next lie, and take the next obedient step.

So when the light comes on again—and it will—don't speed up or look for an exit ramp. Pull over, open the hood, and call on the Master Mechanic to do what only He can.

REFERENCES

Beck, A. T. (1967). *Depression: Clinical, experimental, and theoretical aspects*. Harper & Row.

David, D., Cristea, I., & Hofmann, S. G. (2018). *Why cognitive behavioral therapy is the current gold standard of psychotherapy*. Frontiers in Psychiatry, 9, 4. https://doi.org/10.3389/fpsyt.2018.00004

Doidge, N. (2007). *The brain that changes itself: Stories of personal triumph from the frontiers of brain science*. Viking.

Ellis, A. (1962). *Reason and emotion in psychotherapy*. Lyle Stuart.

Harris, P. L. (1989). *Children and emotion: The development of psychological understanding*. Oxford University Press.

Hebb, D. O. (1949). *The organization of behavior: A neuropsychological theory*. Wiley.

Johnsen, T. J., & Friborg, O. (2015). *The effects of cognitive behavioral therapy as an anti-depressive treatment is falling: A meta-analysis*. Psychological Bulletin, 141(4), 747–768. https://doi.org/10.1037/bul0000015

Lazarus, R. S. (1991). *Emotion and adaptation.* Oxford University Press.

LeDoux, J. E. (1996). *The emotional brain: The mysterious underpinnings of emotional life.* Simon & Schuster.

LeDoux, J. E. (2012). *Rethinking the emotional brain.* Neuron, 73(4), 653–676. https://doi.org/10.1016/j.neuron.2012.02.004

www.ingramcontent.com/pod-product-compliance
Lightning Source LLC
Chambersburg PA
CBHW051441140726
47987CB00006B/2485